Spiritual Direction

Getting You and God Together

Kevin Sharpe

Contents

Introduction

If you've picked up this book, chances are you've heard the phrase *spiritual direction*. It can sound a bit mysterious or even confusing. Maybe you've wondered what it actually is or whether it's something you might need. Is it counseling? Coaching? Prayer? Confession?

It's really none of those things, but in some ways it carries a hint of each. Spiritual direction isn't about someone telling you what to do or fixing problems in your life. It's about having a companion who listens with you and helps you notice how God is showing up in your life. And that's big.

Spiritual direction is a living, relational experience. It's an invitation into more conscious relationship with God, with yourself, with others, and with the world around you.

When you enter that space, something begins to shift. You slow down. You notice the patterns and rhythms already emerging. You begin to see that your life isn't so much about problems to solve but becoming aware of the sacred ground where God is already at work.

At the end of the day, spiritual direction isn't about someone giving you all the answers. Rather, it's more about paying attention. It helps you learn to recognize God's presence in what's most ordinary and sometimes in what's hardest to face. It teaches you how to live awake so that you become more honest, more open, and more receptive to the divine life already moving through you.

People have sought this kind of companionship for centuries. What the spiritual director is called has changed (spiritual friend, soul companion, wise elder), but the heart of spiritual direction is the same: listening together for how God is showing up, and then responding with openness and trust.

This book is for anyone who feels a subtle, or maybe not so subtle, yearning for something deeper. It's for those who are tired of trying to do faith or spirituality alone.

Maybe you're ready to be seen and listened to in a deep way without being judged or controlled.

As you read the following pages, you'll discover that spiritual direction isn't an abstract idea or something reserved for the deeply religious. It's a profoundly human experience that takes shape in ordinary relationship, in simple gestures like listening, pausing, blessing, and being present.

The reflections that follow trace what I call *a living ecology* made up of a landscape of sacred relationships or movements that nurture one another. Each movement—witnessing, blessing, companionship, and trusting presence—offers a glimpse into how God meets you in love and helps you grow in relationship with that love.

You don't have to rush through these pages. Read a little, pause, and let whatever speaks to you stay with you. My hope is that this book meets your curiosity with answers and provides clarity about how spiritual direction can help you and God get together in ways that are honest, grounding, and deeply human.

Part One

1

What Spiritual Direction Really Is (and Isn't)

You know the feeling. That unrelenting "there must be something more" that teases you in times of boredom or overwhelm. It's a restlessness and a craving at the same time.

Spiritual direction begins in that tension. It's a space where you can slow down enough to hear what your life is trying to tell you. It's not about finding quick answers but about making room for the rich conversation already happening on some level between you and God.

Many people first come to spiritual direction because of some inner unsettledness. They sense an undercurrent flowing just below the surface of their life. Some are curious, drawn by a longing they can't quite name. Others arrive weary and bring with them questions about faith, loss, or change. Sometimes it's not about a life struggle. It's about wonder that gives rise to the desire to live with more awareness, to listen for the pulse of the sacred in the ordinary moments.

Whatever the reason, spiritual direction offers a way to listen more deeply to your life, to the world around you, and to God's presence in both.

The word *direction* in *spiritual direction* can be misleading. It sounds like someone is going to tell you what to do or how to live. But spiritual direction isn't that at all. It's not therapy, counseling, or coaching.

In therapy, the focus is often on healing the past. In coaching, it's on achieving goals and shaping what's ahead. In spiritual direction, the focus is on the present: this moment, right here, where God is already near. It's about listening for how the Holy Spirit might be moving in the experiences of your life, often in quiet, easily missed ways.

A spiritual director doesn't give you a plan or tell you what to believe. They don't diagnose or prescribe. Instead, they accompany you. They create a safe, sacred space where you can explore what's arising in your spirit as you begin to understand and trust that the voice you're hearing within may actually be God's.

This process is intentionally unhurried. It moves at the pace of good listening. Sometimes that kind of listening happens in silence. Sometimes it shows up in tears or laughter or stories that you didn't expect to tell.

At its core, spiritual direction is a relationship of deep, honest attention. You bring your life as it is. You speak about your hopes, your confusion, your exhaustion, your desire to be closer to God. And your spiritual director listens with you. Together, you begin to notice where the Spirit of God is flowing and where resistance may be holding you back.

You may speak about prayer that feels hollow or a decision that weighs on you. You may share moments that seem ordinary but keep calling out for your attention. The spiritual director doesn't diagnose what's happening or offer solutions. Instead, they offer something much more profound. They help you notice how your life is connecting to God's ongoing invitation.

The kind of listening that is the hallmark of spiritual direction can be healing in and of itself. It slows the body and softens the mind. It models and teaches you to listen with more than your ears, to sense the movements of your spirit, to pay attention to what rises within when truth is near.

As you continue with spiritual direction, you may start to notice patterns. Maybe you see how peace tends to accompany certain choices. Maybe how joy flickers in unexpected experiences or how God keeps showing up even when you feel lost. Your spiritual director helps you name those moments. They help you see what has always been there just like someone pointing out constellations in a night sky.

Spiritual direction is wholly relational because it mirrors how God meets you: not with pressure or performance, but with presence. A good spiritual director doesn't stand above you but beside you. Together, you practice the art of noticing what is: how God moves, how you respond, how love takes shape in your daily living.

In a culture obsessed with doing and getting more, spiritual direction offers the gift of fully being. It asks you to pause and remember that the spiritual life isn't a project to finish or a ladder to climb. It's a relationship to receive. Meeting with a spiritual director can become an anchor, not a rulebook or a ritual, but a space that keeps you awake to the sacred unfolding in the midst of everyday life.

And in that awakening, something begins to shift. The questions don't always disappear, but they draw you in. The striving gives way as you begin to realize that God was never as far away as you thought. Spiritual direction helps you come home to that truth.

With spiritual direction, you don't seek to become someone new or set out to reach an "ideal" level of faith. You enter into the relationship of spiritual direction to become more authentically yourself: the person God already loves, the one who's been seen and named "beloved" from the beginning.

If you've ever wanted a relationship where you can bring your questions without fear of being judged, where silence feels safe and presence feels real, spiritual direction may be what you've been searching for. It's good to remember that you don't have to know exactly what you're looking for. You only need a little curiosity and the willingness to be honest about where you are.

Spiritual direction is, at its core, a sacred conversation: two people listening together for how God is at work in one life—yours.

2

Listening for the Holy

HAVE YOU EVER BEEN with someone who truly listens? Not with someone waiting for their turn to talk or rushing to fill the silence. But with someone who pays attention to your words, your pauses, even the unspoken stories that live beneath them. That kind of listening changes the atmosphere. It gives you room to breathe. You begin to hear yourself in a new way.

This kind of listening gives life to spiritual direction. It has a different rhythm from most conversations. There is no intention to solve a specific problem, no advice waiting to be given, no pressure to perform. It is two people moving toward what is real, listening together for how God is present.

You might find yourself surrounded by distraction. Notifications. Conversations. Endless tasks that fill the hours of the day. You might stay busy, keeping pace with the day, while your inner life often trails behind. This can make it difficult to hear what you truly feel or know. Spiritual direction slows the pace. It creates room for what has been lost in the noise to surface.

You may notice things you have ignored for a long time. A question that will not go away. A memory that keeps returning. A longing that waits to be noticed. None of these things need to be solved or explained. They simply need space and air to breathe. And it is in this space that you learn to stop trying to manage everything. It is in this space that you discover that God is fully present and waiting for you to notice, to become aware.

Your spiritual director helps you with this process of leaning into this space where life is so alive. They help you stay open to all that is moving just underneath the surface of your life. They do not analyze or interpret for you. They help you pay attention. Their calm steadiness allows you to stay with what is real instead of trying to find and cling to easy answers. With them beside you, what feels ordinary begins to reveal its richness.

At first, this way of listening can feel unfamiliar. Most people are used to fast conversations and quick results. In spiritual direction, silence becomes a partner in the process. It encourages reflection. Sometimes it brings something surprising: a realization, a genuine smile, a memory that finally makes sense.

Listening for the holy is not about escaping your life or chasing big spiritual moments. It is about learning to see that God is already living in the details of your days. When you give listening your full attention, it becomes an act of prayer. You do not need perfect words. You only need to show up and be present.

With the help of your spiritual director, you begin to hear your own life differently. You notice what brings calm and what creates tension. You sense when peace settles in and when resistance holds you back. These movements may be faint, like whispers, but they become familiar.

They make up the language God often uses to speak to you.

Your spiritual director helps you learn that language. They might ask simple questions like, "What do you notice as you say that?" or "Where do you feel that in your body?" These are not questions to be solved but doorways to enter and explore what's showing up within.

When you bear witness like this, your life becomes a teacher. You begin to trust that God is not waiting somewhere beyond reach. The divine meets you where you already are. It meets you in the middle of your story, your work, your confusion, your hope. You get in a very embodied way that the sacred has always been close.

And so, being listened to in this way during spiritual direction ends up changing how you actually listen to yourself and others. You become more patient with your life. You stop trying to force clarity. You begin to allow understanding to come to light at its own pace and in its own time. You start to see that what you long for may already be here, now, just waiting to be recognized.

This is what listening for the holy in spiritual direction offers. It helps you live from a place of open awareness rather than from a need for control. It reminds you that prayer and life are not separate things. They are one holy expression, and even the smallest moments begin to carry meaning.

After a spiritual direction session, the world around you may look the same, but something inside you has shifted. It may be almost imperceptible, yet it starts to open your awareness to the ways God has been near all along.

Let's remember that spiritual direction is not about mastering a new skill or learning a special method. It is about remembering in a real and experiential way what is already true. God meets you right where you are, in stillness and in conversation, in the ordinary moments of your life.

3

An Ecology of Relationship

Everything in life is connected. You sense this when you step into the forest or walk by the ocean. Each sound, color, and breath belongs to something larger. The same is true in your spiritual life. Spiritual direction helps you notice that connection, not as an idea to understand, but as something you live every day.

Fundamentally, it invites you to see that your relationship with God is not separate from how you relate to yourself, to others, and to the world around you. When you grow in awareness of one, you inevitably touch the others. The way you listen to God shapes the way you listen to people. The way you care for your inner life influences the way you care for the earth.

In spiritual direction, this truth becomes personal and tangible. You might come in thinking you're talking about your prayer life, but as you speak, you begin to notice the patterns that shape your relationship with God and with others.

Most of these patterns are rooted in trust, fear, or desire. Spiritual direction helps you see how they are woven together into the fabric of your relationships, revealing the intricate ways your life and relationships are interconnected.

A spiritual director helps you see those connections. They listen not only for what you say, but for what lives behind your words. They might notice how your tone changes when you talk about something that brings peace, or how your body shifts when you speak of something that feels heavy. Their attention is not analysis. It is care. It helps you see how God is already at work in the flow of relationship itself.

Everything in spiritual direction happens within relationship. This is what makes it more than a conversation about faith. It becomes a living expression of it. You are not learning information about God. You are entering a way of relating that mirrors God's own way of being in relationship. With patience. With understanding. And with love that does not demand perfection.

When you begin to see your life through this lens, everything starts to look different. You realize that God's presence is not limited to prayer or worship. It shows up in the way you speak to a friend, how you treat your own body, how you notice beauty in a regular day. Spiritual direction helps you recognize that the sacred is not hidden somewhere else; it is embedded into the very structure of your life.

This awareness begins to change how you move through the world. You become more patient with yourself, less reactive with others, more attuned to the natural world that sustains you. You start to see that you are part of a larger whole, and that God's love moves through all of it.

Spiritual direction reminds you that transformation rarely happens in isolation. It takes shape in and through relationship, where listening deepens, where honesty becomes possible, and where love takes root. In that sense, spiritual direction is not a separate practice; it is part of the larger ecology of life itself, a way of living that keeps you connected to God and to everything that is alive.

Part Two

4

The Living Landscape of Spiritual Direction

IF THE FIRST PART of this book has helped you understand what spiritual direction is, this next part will show you how it actually unfolds. These chapters offer a glimpse inside the experience of spiritual direction, revealing the qualities that create the space of deep listening that helps you see how God is already moving in your life.

Think of this section as entering a landscape, miraculously alive and vibrant. Streams flow into one another. Each one has its own character, yet together they form a single ecosystem of relationship and grace.

This analogy of a landscape works well. It shines light on the fact that spiritual direction isn't a set of steps to follow or lessons to master. It's a living relationship that moves and breathes. The spiritual director listens and responds, not from a script, but from an attentive posture that honors what is happening in the moment. Sometimes that looks like stillness. Sometimes it looks like naming what is sacred. Sometimes it looks like carrying something challenging together with you or trusting what is ready to emerge.

The four streams (or movements) within this living landscape are witnessing, blessing, companionship, and trusting presence. Each reveals a different facet of how a spiritual director shows up and how God meets you in that shared space.

As you spend time with the next four chapters, you'll see how each movement takes shape through a story from the Gospels. These stories aren't offered as instruction but as reflection, providing context and tone. They show what spiritual direction looks like when it's lived and embodied, and how that makes room for divine encounter.

5

The Witness

THE RIVER MOVES SLOWLY. Its water curls around John's legs. The heat of the day presses in on him. The sounds of birds echo from the reeds. He takes a moment to breathe. Then he looks up and sees Jesus approaching through the dust. Something in the air shifts. It is not dramatic, just a subtle awareness that the moment has weight.

John watches as Jesus enters the water. John feels the open space give over to the closeness of Jesus now standing next to him. He looks into Jesus's eyes. A moment more and he takes a deep breath that is both a pause of recognition and a way of filling himself with reverence for the mystery before him.

"I need to be baptized by you," he says, as Jesus moves in closer.

Both men stand in the same current, water moving around their bodies, the air alive with expectancy. John remains steady and present. He is attentive to what is unfolding before him. When Jesus rises from the river, the Holy Spirit descends. A voice speaks of belovedness, and John stands in silence, aware that something holy has been revealed.

❖

The first movement within the living landscape of spiritual direction is the art of witnessing.

John does not make the holy appear in this moment at the river. He recognizes it. He doesn't interpret or explain. He simply sees what is already taking place. That kind of seeing requires stillness and attention. The same is true in spiritual direction. The spiritual director does not create the encounter with God. They hold space for it, watching with reverence as the movement of God reveals itself in your life.

Witnessing is more than observation. It is a form of participation that comes from listening carefully and openly.

When you are listened to in this way, you begin to hear your own life differently. You start to notice where God has been moving all along.

The spiritual director listens alongside you. They help you stay with what is unfolding, rather than rushing to make sense of it. Together, you learn that witnessing means being fully with someone, staying present in the midst of whatever the moment brings.

Most people live by analysis. They want to understand, name, and categorize what is happening. But witnessing asks for something different. It asks for openness to what is not yet understood. In spiritual direction, this means staying close to the mystery of your own story. It means staying in the current long enough to notice where God is at work.

The spiritual director practices this kind of witnessing with you. It takes courage to stay still and remain steady when the urge arises to explain. It takes trust to look at what is uncertain. It takes even more trust to allow it to speak in its own time. The witness does not hurry what is becoming. They hold it with care until it begins to take shape.

In spiritual direction, bearing witness is what allows transformation to happen naturally. When you are seen without judgment, something inside you begins to rest. When your story is received with compassion instead of critique, you begin to see yourself through the same lens of mercy. That is how awareness develops.

The body responds to this kind of awareness. It relaxes in compassion, leans in with curiosity, and opens in wonder. This is what it means to be fully present: to trust that God can hold what is still becoming and to offer your whole self as witness to that work.

You need someone who can see you clearly and hold who you are becoming with compassion. The spiritual director accomplishes this not by solving problems or giving advice, but by bearing witness. They are a companion who helps reveal the pattern of God's work in your life, often before you can see it yourself. Through this process, both the spiritual director and the directee learn to see more clearly.

To bear witness is to honor what is holy in another. It is to notice where the divine is showing up and to name it with reverence. It is to say, sometimes without words, *"I see God here, in you."*

The miracle at the Jordan did not depend on John, but it happened in his presence. So it is with spiritual direction. Transformation unfolds in the sure company of one who is present, who stands beside you, and who sees what is already alive.

This seeing of the sacred that is already here, waiting to be recognized, is the work of witness.

6

The Blessing

As Elizabeth steps forward to greet Mary, she notices a slight tremble in Mary's hand as she brushes a few strands of stray hair away from her cheek. Then the quick rise and fall of her breath from the journey. The moment their eyes meet, the child in Elizabeth's womb kicks, and something within her awakens.

In that instant, awareness deepens. Elizabeth listens to what she feels within her heart and gives it voice. "Blessed are you among women, and blessed is the fruit of your womb."

◈

The meeting between these two women is more than a family reunion. It is a sacred moment of response. Through Elizabeth, affirmation takes voice. Through Mary, that affirmation is received. Elizabeth doesn't analyze what is happening or try to make sense of it. She simply allows what she feels to become language. Her blessing doesn't explain the mystery making itself known. It honors it.

This is what happens in spiritual direction when recognition turns into response. Once the spiritual director begins to see where God is moving in another person's life, the next step is blessing. It is the act of naming what is good and true, not to label or define it, but to affirm it. It is the humble, sacred response of one who has seen something holy begin to take shape and chooses to speak life into that awareness. The spiritual director doesn't add anything new. They reflect what is already there.

In spiritual direction, blessing often sounds like a spacious noticing. "You seem at peace as you talk about that." "There's light in your face when you remember that moment." These reflections are not compliments. They are invitations for the directee to pause and take in what has been revealed. They help make the invisible visible. Blessing is the language of affirmation that draws attention to what God is doing.

Elizabeth shows us that blessing is not abstract or detached. It is embodied. She feels before she speaks. Her words rise from within her, from the same place where the Holy Spirit is moving. Her whole being participates in the encounter, not only her voice but her awareness, her presence, her care. Blessing flows from that deep attentiveness. It is not always joy. Sometimes blessing acknowledges pain or sorrow, grief or uncertainty. To bless is to hold what is, to affirm that God is present within it, whatever form it takes.

The sacred often reveals itself in this way. It doesn't come through explanation but through experience. A stillness that fills the room. A tear that surprises. A sense of calm assurance that arrives unannounced. A spiritual director pays attention to those moments and honors them with presence. They might ask, "What do you sense God is saying in this?" or they might simply hold space for silence, letting the truth speak for itself. In these ways, blessing is given form. It's not by teaching or telling, but by bearing witness to what is unfolding, and then affirming it as good.

These moments cannot be forced or manufactured. They come freely and often when least expected. And they always seem to arrive at the right time. The spiritual director's role is to stay present and responsive, to make space for another to recognize what they already carry within. Blessing deepens awareness not by adding new insight but by giving voice to what is already true.

Blessing is not about comfort or flattery. It is about helping someone remember that the divine is moving within their story. It gives shape to the truth that the sacred is personal, near, and active. Sometimes this is expressed in words, sometimes through tone or gesture, but always through presence that honors what is holy in another.

When you sit with a spiritual director who blesses in this way, you begin to trust what is awakening within you. Their presence doesn't inflate or diminish your experience. It holds it with care, helping you see that God's movement is not fragile or fleeting, but steady and real. Blessing becomes a way of saying, "*What is happening in you matters. God is here.*"

Blessing, then, is bigger than shared joy. It is shared awareness. It happens in the space between two people who are listening together and choosing to name what is true. It reminds them that they don't have to create holiness. They only have to notice it and give it voice.

7

The Companion

THE ROAD IS CROWDED. Loud. Feet shuffle too close. Voices jeer. Simon catches sight of the condemned man. Stumbling, he struggles to carry the heavy crossbeam. And then, the hard grip of hands seizes Simon. Soldiers pull him through the crowd. He knows better than to resist. He is shoved against the man and rises up to meet the weight of the beam.

Step by step, he falls into rhythm beside the man. Their shoulders bump against each other. The weight of the cross-beam shifts between them. Neither speaks. They simply walk, the weight shared, and their silence holding what words cannot.

❖

Simon of Cyrene did not choose this moment, but he did not turn away from it either. He entered the mystery of shared experience—the unflinching flow of presence that holds space for the experience. This is another stream within the living landscape of spiritual direction: the art of compassionate accompaniment.

There are times in spiritual direction when joy and clarity fill the conversation, but there are also moments when sorrow or confusion draws near. During these heavier times, the spiritual director does not pull away or rush toward resolution. They stay beside you and whatever heaviness that shows up. Their work is not to lift the weight but to share it through steady presence.

Compassion in spiritual direction is not sentimental. It isn't pity or reaction to make pain disappear. It is a presence that abides. While listening opens space for what is sacred to be noticed, this same act of listening carries with it the quality of steadfastness. The spiritual director stays present when words fall short and grief or confusion fills the room. Their calm attention steadies. It assures the directee that they are not alone in their pain.

This kind of accompaniment is fully embodied. It slows the pace of conversation and roots it in presence. The spiritual director's calm helps the other person find their own footing. A deep breath replaces a rush of words. A silence becomes a resting place. Compassion is carried in posture, in tone, in the willingness to stay when everything else feels too much.

When someone meets you in this way, without judgment or solutions, something begins to shift. You start to trust that your pain is not too much to hold. You sense that God is near, not as a distant observer, but as one who bears the weight with you. Spiritual direction becomes an experience where suffering is not erased but met with openness.

Simon's story shows that accompaniment is not about choosing suffering but about refusing to turn away from it. He steps into another's burden and stays close through the weight of it. That is the heart of the spiritual director's calling: to recognize God's presence even in the hard places and to remain long enough for it to be seen.

In spiritual direction, this may look like sitting in silence while someone weeps, or staying calm while a painful truth surfaces. It may mean allowing the mystery of suffering to exist without being compelled to explain it. The spiritual director's presence communicates something essential. It reveals that the love of God is wide enough to include even this moment.

Gradually, the one carrying the weight begins to notice that they are not carrying it alone. The very act of being accompanied gives room for strength to rise. While companionship does not remove the crossbeam, it changes how it is carried. It makes known that pain is not the end of the story.

The spiritual director remains grounded and trustworthy in this stream of accompaniment. They hold space with compassion and reverence, trusting that God is near. Their steadiness helps the directee to stay. To breathe. To begin sensing God's presence within their own experience of suffering and to discover that even in carrying heavy burdens, they are not alone.

8

The Trusting Presence

MARY WATCHES. LISTENS. THE wedding feast overflows with noise. With laughter. The guests mingle with cups in hand and unaware that the wine has run out. Only Mary notices the lack. She turns to her son, "They have no wine." She listens to him. And as their eyes meet in the brief silence that follows, something passes between them. This time unspoken. A knowing that runs deeper than words, touching the heart of both mother and son. Then she turns to the servants and says simply, "Do whatever he tells you." The jars are filled, water drawn and poured. Somewhere in the action of obedience, water becomes wine.

◈

This is story is not about grand gestures or dramatic miracles. It begins with an ordinary moment. Mary notices what others overlook. She doesn't panic. She simply names what is true and trusts that her part is to stay available.

That posture of trust and availability lies at the heart of spiritual direction. The spiritual director, like Mary, learns to notice what has run dry in another's life, where joy has faded, where energy feels thin, where hope has lost its color. The director doesn't rush to fill those empty spaces with solutions. Instead, they hold them with subtle confidence, helping the other person rest in the assurance that God is already at work, even when nothing yet seems to change.

In spiritual direction, emptiness is not a failure to be corrected. It's an opening to be honored. It is in the space where something runs out that God's transforming work often begins. Naming that truth is an act of courage. Holding it without anxiety is an act of trust.

Mary models both. She names the lack—"They have no

wine"—and then steps back. Her trust is not passive resignation. It's active availability, a readiness to respond when the time comes. The spiritual director embodies the same stance: open, patient, attentive, creating space for grace to move in its own rhythm.

This work requires more than listening. It calls for an interior trust, a grounded presence that says without words, "We can stay here. We can wait together." In that kind of space, the directee begins to breathe differently. They realize they do not have to perform or prove anything. They can just be where they are and trust that the sacred is already near.

The servants in the story show what availability looks like in action. They don't understand the whole plan. They just do what is asked. They fill the jars with water, carry them, pour them. Simple, faithful movement. Transformation happens within that obedience. No one sees the moment water changes to wine. The miracle is hidden within the process of participation.

In spiritual direction, it's much the same. The conversation unfolds slowly. Questions rise and settle. The spiritual director helps the directee stay with what is present, to keep showing up even when clarity has not yet come. Over time, trust deepens. Availability grows. Small moments of awareness start to fill with meaning.

The spiritual director offers unwavering presence rather than intervention. Their calm attention helps the directee find the courage to stay with what is unfolding. Over time, the directee begins to see that God's work doesn't depend on blind effort but on willingness to be present.

This is the movement of trust and availability working together. Trust opens the heart to God's presence. Availability keeps it open so that transformation can take root. When both are held with care, life begins to shift from striving to surrender, from effort to participation.

Spiritual direction, at its best, helps you live from this place. It teaches you to notice the lacks without judgment, to name them honestly, and to remain open to what God might be doing through them. The spiritual director's role is not to guide from ahead but to stand beside, affirming that divine movement is already unfolding.

At Cana, the miracle did not depend on Mary's command or the servants' skills. It happened in their presence, through their trust, their availability, and their willingness to do what was asked of them. And somewhere within the ordinary rhythm of noticing, naming, and waiting, water becomes wine.

Part Three

9

From Listening to Living

Spiritual direction doesn't end in the room where it takes place. What happens there begins to move outward, shaping how you live and relate in the rest of your life. Every conversation, every pause, every moment of shared noticing opens something in you. It teaches you to live with a little more awareness, a little more compassion, a little more trust.

Through the earlier chapters, you've learned about the living landscape of spiritual direction. You've examined how witnessing, blessing, accompaniment, and trusting presence co-create a sacred rhythm of listening and being listened to. Each of these movements helps you notice how God is already at work in your life. But this awareness is only the beginning. What you begin to recognize in spiritual direction slowly begins to influence and shape the way you live in the world.

The qualities that make spiritual direction so transformative are the same ones that help you live in deeper relationship with God, with yourself, and with the people around you. In spiritual direction, you begin to learn what it really means to show up honestly and respond to the ways the divine moves in your life. Along the way, these qualities shape each of these relationships in meaningful ways.

In this next part of the book, you'll explore those relationships more closely. This exploration begins with the relationship that grounds all the rest: your relationship with God. From there, you'll look at how experiencing that divine love transforms your relationship with yourself and then with the world around you. Each of these relationships reflects and deepens the others, forming a kind of holy ecosystem.

So as you turn to these next chapters, think of them as a window into what spiritual direction makes possible. What begins in a real conversation between two people ripples outward into the way you live life. The insights discovered in spiritual direction take shape in real relationships: with God, with yourself, and with others. This is where the practice of spiritual direction meets the practice of everyday life.

10

Relationship With God

Jesus steps slowly into the river and notices the cool water against his skin. The air vibrates with life and expectation. The smell of earth and water holds the moment for what comes next.

Now, he closes his eyes and relaxes into John's arms. Before a thought can form, he is beneath the surface of the water. Time pauses in the hush of water and breath. No crowd. No task. No mission. Only stillness. Then John lifts him from the river. Light breaks across the surface, and the sky seems to open with a steady, unhurried voice: "You are my beloved Son; with you I am well pleased."

The words ripple through his body. They do not instruct or demand. They do not ask for proof or performance. They name what has always been true.

Still resting in John's arms, Jesus receives this truth, and his whole being absorbs it.

❖

This is how relationship with God begins: not with doing, but with receiving. This moment in the river's water instructs that divine love comes first. Before Jesus heals, teaches, or sacrifices anything, he hears that he is loved. That truth is the ground beneath everything that follows.

In spiritual direction, you return to that same truth. Each session becomes a space to remember what has already been spoken: that you are seen, known, and loved by God. The spiritual director doesn't give you this truth. They help you notice it again. Sometimes it arrives in words, sometimes in the felt experience of your body, sometimes in the awareness that you are not alone.

You may know, at least in theory, that God loves you. But do you always trust it? Do you treat love like something you must earn by being good, wise, or faithful enough? In spiritual direction, the beliefs that block the reality that God loves you begin to soften. The conversation itself becomes a reminder that you already have God's attention and love. You don't have to earn it or deserve it. You simply allow yourself to receive it.

Your spiritual director helps you practice this. They stay with you in the places where faith feels uncertain or prayer feels empty. They don't spend time filling the silence or repairing what feels broken. Their presence conveys the truth that God's love has not gone anywhere.

Receiving love is not easy. It asks for control to be let go of. It asks for you to allow yourself to be held. You, like so many, may be far more comfortable giving love than receiving it. But spiritual direction invites you to stay open, even when it feels uncomfortable, until you begin to believe that love does not depend on your performance. It simply is.

Moments of this awareness often arrive without fanfare. A long breath. A wave of peace. A memory that settles in a new way. These are the signs that belovedness is taking root. They do not come through striving but through stillness. The spiritual director helps you notice and name them, so they can continue to emerge.

Gradually, your relationship with God begins to change. Prayer feels less like a duty and more like a home-coming. You find yourself talking to God, not as some judge but as pure loving and accepting presence. The restless drive to "get it right" gives way to a comfortable rhythm of trust.

Spiritual direction nurtures a relationship grounded in love that makes no demands. It is not something to achieve, but a place to live from. When you rest in your belovedness, you begin to see that love from God is not the reward for the journey. It is the starting point.

11

Relationship With Self

THE DESERT HOLDS AN unquiet silence. The wind howls over the land. Stones crack under the sun and the cold of night, sending tiny pops into the stillness. Pebbles crunch underfoot. For forty days, Jesus walks this landscape of emptiness: sun on his shoulders, the taste of salt and thirst on his lips, his own breath harsh and labored. This kind of silence is relentless. It isolates and overcomes.

Hunger settles deep into his body. Now, a voice drifts near, sure and insistent. "If you are the Son of God..." The words reverberate as they try to destabilize and dislodge his very identity.

Jesus stands in the desert and listens. He does not argue or defend. He lets the command hang in the dry air, testing its weight against his own heart: Who am I when the affirmation fades, when the hunger rises, when I have nothing left to hold but myself? The wilderness becomes a mirror. Each shadow, each echo, shows what he might cling to—power, recognition, control. Slowly, the truth that was spoken earlier ("Beloved") shines out from his heart. What is false begins to fall away. What remains is the bright awareness of who he is and whose he is.

❖

This is the work of relationship with self: to stay present to what is real, to see both strength and weakness without turning away. It is not a search for perfection, but an honest meeting with what lives within you.

In spiritual direction, this kind of meeting takes shape through shared reflection. It is not about analysis or self-improvement. It is about becoming familiar with your own inner landscape. The spiritual director serves as a calm, grounded presence, helping you notice how you move through your experiences. This is how you give space to where you hide, what you avoid, what calls you forward. Together, you begin to name what is true.

Naming brings clarity. It lets what has been hidden step into the light, not to be judged, but to be known. You might begin to see how certain patterns or stories have shaped your way of being. You might recognize how fear or shame still speaks louder than truth. The goal is not to erase those voices but to recognize them for what they are. When they are seen, they lose their power to define you.

Spiritual direction offers the space for this kind of honest seeing. The spiritual director does not tell you who you are. They simply help you look long enough to remember. You learn that the parts of yourself you once pushed aside are not barriers to God but places where God is waiting to meet you. The more you accept what is within, the more you recognize how deeply you are loved.

This growing self-awareness becomes a doorway to connection. You begin to live less from reaction and more from grounding. You speak to yourself with the same acceptance your spiritual director offers you. You begin to treat your own heart as something sacred. That shift changes everything.

When you begin to trust yourself in this way, you also begin to trust God more deeply. You realize that God's love has never depended on your perfection. It has always moved through the full reality of who you are, including your doubts, your longings, your limitations, and your gifts.

This discovery comes to light slowly in spiritual direction. You learn to see yourself through God's eyes, not as something broken to repair but as a person to cherish. You begin to understand that being known by God and knowing yourself are not separate movements. They are part of the same flow of love.

The wilderness, once a place of testing, becomes a place of belonging. It is where you learn that love does not demand success or certainty. It only asks for honesty. And in that honesty, you find freedom.

12

Relationship With Others

THE SUN SITS HIGH in a cloudless sky. Heat presses on her shoulders. She treads the familiar path toward the well just outside the village. The ring of stone waits ahead, holding a small circle of shade. Her jar rests steady against her hip. She keeps her eyes low, hoping for a moment alone.

But as soon as she looks up, she sees him.

A man rests beside the well, dust on his sandals, travel worn, motionless in the heat. She feels her steps slow. A Jewish man, here, at this hour. Every practiced boundary rises inside her. She breathes in deeply, steadying herself, and continues forward.

As she nears the well, he looks up. His gaze meets hers without judgment or dismissal. "Will you give me a drink?"

The question unsettles her. It crosses the line that keeps their worlds apart. Confusion floods her mind. And then out of nowhere: the pull of being seen. She hesitates. She wants to run, but her feet hold still. She sets the water jar down.

❖

The conversation begins with ordinary things: water, thirst, the heat of the day. Then it deepens, and what separates them thins. He names what is true about her life, not to condemn, but to reveal that even here, in the middle of her ordinary day, God is already near. The jar in her hands, once a symbol of burden, becomes a sign of awakening. When she sets it down, she no longer hides.

This encounter is not only about her story. It is about what happens between them. It is about the space that opens when one person is willing to meet another with honesty and respect. That space, fragile yet holy, becomes the birthplace of transformation.

Spiritual direction carries this same kind of sacred space into the life of relationship. It reminds us that what passes between two people, such as attention, compassion, and truth, can be a channel for grace. Relationship is more than understanding each other. It is about honoring what takes place between each other.

The experience of spiritual direction teaches this through presence. When a spiritual director receives you with steadiness and openness, you begin to feel what it means to be met rather than managed. Their unspoken acceptance gives you room. You can let your full self show up, even what feels uncertain or unfinished. That kind of welcome transforms. It begins to shape how you meet others.

You start to notice when presence matters more than persuasion, when respect runs deeper than agreement, when compassion can hold difference without needing to erase it. What begins as an experience in spiritual direction becomes a way of moving through the world.

This shift is not something you force. It grows naturally as you internalize what you have experienced in spiritual direction. The spiritual director's trust in God's presence becomes your own. You begin to believe that grace can hold both your life and the lives of those around you. This trust helps you stay open. even when understanding is incomplete or when connection feels fragile.

It may take some time, but this becomes how you show up for others. You listen with more patience. You speak with greater kindness. You embody the knowing that compassion and love do not need to control. You find that the sacred is not confined to spiritual settings. It lives in the silence between words and in the shared laughter and the forgiving gesture that arrives when least expected.

The woman at the well left her jar behind when she discovered something greater than the water she came to fill it with. Her encounter became a testimony of having been seen and loved. Every relationship offers that same possibility.

Spiritual direction helps you live from that place. It shows you how to meet another with the kind of reverence that allows grace to move freely between you. In that shared space, love becomes something tangible, something you can receive, something you can offer, something that can heal the world.

Part Four

13

The Life that Unfolds

MANY PEOPLE DESCRIBE THEIR experience of spiritual direction and its effects as subtle at first. There's usually no grand revelation or dramatic change. Rather, it's a gradual sort of awakening. You might start to notice how you pause before reacting, how you breathe differently when someone speaks, how you carry a deeper sense of being grounded. These are not separate from prayer or faith. They are the slow work of becoming more awake to the divine presence woven through the ordinary moments of life.

Spiritual direction was never meant to exist apart from the rest of life. It teaches you a way of seeing and being that reaches into everything. It opens your eyes to the way you treat your body. You start to see how you make choices. And you become keenly aware of how you meet both joy and struggle. The posture learned in spiritual direction, this openness and attentiveness, slowly becomes part of who you are.

In this way, spiritual direction facilitates an integration, a bringing together of what might once have felt divided: your inner life and your outer actions, your spiritual questions and your daily responsibilities, your prayer and your work. It's not about achieving balance as much as discovering a natural rhythm where everything belongs.

The chapters that follow explore how this develops, looking at how spiritual direction moves from an hour in a room out into the rest of your life. You'll also find guidance if you feel drawn to seek out spiritual direction for yourself.

14

The Body as a Listening Place

THE BODY OFTEN KNOWS things long before the mind can explain them. A sudden tightness in the chest. A deep sigh. A knot in the stomach. These are signs that something within you wants to be heard. Spiritual direction helps you pay attention to those signals and trust that they matter.

When you meet with a spiritual director, you bring more than your words. You bring your whole self. Every movement, every pause, every shift in tone carries meaning. The spiritual director doesn't only listen to what you say but also to how your body says it. The body becomes a kind of guide, offering clues about about how God is moving in your life.

This may be a new idea for you. For many, it is. You may not have been taught to see your body in this way. You may have learned to think of spirituality as something that happens in the mind or heart, separate from flesh and bone. But in spiritual direction, the body is not a distraction from spirituality; it's part of it. A clenched jaw may reveal unspoken fear. Shoulders drawn tight may signal a burden that's gone unshared. A tear may show up before the words ever do. The body begins to speak its stories, and awareness begins to listen.

This kind of listening takes practice. You, like so many, may spend much of life in your head, trying to figure things out. In spiritual direction, you learn to slow down. If your breath changes or you suddenly go quiet, your spiritual director may ask, "What's happening right now?" It's not analysis. It's an invitation to notice. Often that pause in the conversation opens a door. A feeling rises. A truth surfaces. Awareness moves from thought into something felt and real and unfiltered.

This embodied awareness changes how you experience faith. It reminds you that spirituality is not an escape from being human but a deeper way of entering into it. Each breath, each sensation, each heartbeat becomes part of a sacred conversation continually taking place below the surface of your mind.

As awareness deepens, you begin to notice how your body responds to truth. Peace feels spacious. Anxiety feels small and tight. Joy feels open and alive. The more you notice your body, the more you learn to trust these inner movements. They help you recognize what aligns with love and what does not. It isn't about perfection. It's about presence. It's about letting your whole self participate in knowing that God is near.

The body also teaches humility. It keeps you honest when your mind wants to run ahead. It grounds you when life feels scattered. It reminds you that God meets you in real time, in this physical world, not somewhere outside of it.

As you grow more aware of how your body carries experience through spiritual direction, you start to notice those same cues everywhere. How you breathe before a hard conversation. How your shoulders relax when you feel safe. How a deep exhale follows surrender. The body becomes a companion in discernment, a steady reminder that God's presence is not distant or abstract but here, now, and alive in you.

15

Silence, Breath, and the Ordinary

MOST OF LIFE HAPPENS in the small moments. Making coffee. Folding laundry. Standing in line at the grocery store. These moments don't look particularly spiritual, yet they hold more weight than you think. What spiritual direction helps you see is that the ordinary isn't separate from the sacred. It's where the sacred hides in plain sight.

During a spiritual direction session, you begin to slow down enough to notice this. The spaces between words, a deep breath, a sudden silence that feels full instead of empty. These moments can train your attention. They can teach you that presence doesn't require candles or perfect stillness. It just asks for awareness.

That kind of awareness or noticing begins to follow you into the rest of your life. You start to feel when your breath shortens in stressful situations or when your body relaxes when you stop trying to control an outcome. You notice your reactions a little sooner. You notice stillness that once went unnoticed. The same attention you practice in spiritual direction starts to show up in ordinary moments.

As this deepens, spiritual direction begins to shape how you live. You discover that relationship with the divine is not limited to prayer or reflection. It shows up in a smile, in a long exhale, even in the way you wait at a stoplight. Each breath becomes part of the shared connection between you and God. Inhale, receive. Exhale, offer. Slowly, this becomes less a technique and more the way you move through the world.

Spiritual direction doesn't turn you into a monastic or a mystic. It helps you become more alive to what's already taking place. You begin to see how grace moves through your actual life—not a future one, not a more polished one, but the life you already are living. The dishes, the emails, the walks outside, the hesitations before hard words. All of it becomes the ground where awareness grows.

There will still be noise and hurry and distraction. But with the help of spiritual direction, you will carry a different kind of attention. You will begin to notice what used to blur by. You will start to sense when the moment is asking for a deep breath, when silence has more to share than words, when a small act of kindness carries the weight of prayer.

Spiritual direction helps you lean into trusting that holiness is not rare. It is steady and continual. It lives in the flow of your breath, in the texture of your days, and in the space between one heartbeat and the next. This is the ordinary life, made luminous not by perfection, but by presence.

16

Beginning with a Spiritual Director

SOMETIMES SOMETHING INSIDE YOU shifts. It isn't loud or dramatic. It's more like an inner noticing that keeps tapping your shoulder and saying *There's something more here.* That's often how people find their way to spiritual direction. Not through a plan, but by paying attention to that inner nudge.

You don't have to be certain about spiritual direction or spiritually advanced to start. You don't even have to know what to say. Curiosity is enough. If you've ever wanted someone to listen without judgment, or wondered how to sense God's presence in the middle of your real, everyday life, then you're already on your way.

Finding a spiritual director is less about a list of credentials and more about fit. You're looking for someone who listens well, who carries a grounded faith, and who can hold space without trying to manage or steer your journey. A trustworthy spiritual director won't hand you conclusions. They'll help you notice God's presence in your real life.

You can often find spiritual directors through retreat centers, seminaries, or local faith communities. Many also meet with people online. Read a few profiles, ask for recommendations, and don't hesitate to meet with more than one person during your search. It's also worth giving the relationship several sessions before making a decision. It can take time to relax into the rhythm of spiritual direction and to know whether you feel seen, safe, and supported.

Your first session may be simple. You'll talk a little about what drew you to spiritual direction and what you hope for. The spiritual director will likely explain how they work and what to expect. This is the space and time for honesty and exploration. You can bring whatever feels alive: questions, confusion, gratitude, exhaustion, hope. All of it belongs.

Most people meet with a spiritual director once a month for about an hour. Sessions move at their own pace, and often slowly. There may be questions or moments of quiet, but nothing is rushed. Sometimes you'll talk about prayer or a decision you're facing. Sometimes you'll just trace where you've noticed a shift in your heart. The spiritual director may ask questions or invite silence to settle for a moment before speaking. Those pauses can become the most meaningful part of the conversation.

You don't have to prepare much for a spiritual direction session. What helps most is openness. Notice what's been on your mind and heart. Notice what's felt heavy or beautiful or confusing. Bring those things. After several sessions, you'll begin to notice how they form a rhythm of reflection that help you live life with more awareness.

A good spiritual director will never push an agenda or force a conclusion. They'll listen for what's true and help you do the same. Sometimes you'll leave with clarity.

Other times you won't, yet you'll still feel more settled inside. Both are gifts. The work of spiritual direction isn't about arriving at answers. It's about learning to live inside relationship—with God, with yourself, with others.

When you notice that inner awareness calling you, perhaps nudging you toward spiritual direction, let it guide your next step.

About the Author

Kevin Sharpe is a spiritual director, educator, and writer who accompanies people as they find their way back into relationship with God. Through one-on-one spiritual direction, retreats, workshops, and writing, he offers a grounded and compassionate approach that honors both the body and the lived human experience.

Kevin's work centers on the belief that healing and transformation happen through relationship—with God, with ourselves, and with others. Making use of imagination- and body-based contemplative practices, he helps people listen for how the Holy Spirit is already present in their daily lives.

Many of those Kevin companions are healing from religious wounding or spiritual disconnection. Others come simply longing for a more authentic and embodied relationship with God. Wherever they begin, the work is the same: slowing down, paying attention, and discovering that grace meets us exactly where we are.

Kevin also teaches centering prayer and discernment skills, supporting both individuals and communities who are ready to explore deeper, healthier ways of being with God and one another.

To learn more or inquire about spiritual direction, visit www.kevinsharpe.org.